**Jafeth Mariani**

# MEOW ZEN

You are pure freedom

AF221200

# MEOW ZEN

## You are pure freedom

Jafeth Mariani

Metaphors and spiritual exercises
to feel better instantly

Original drawings: Jafeth Mariani

Bibliografische Information der Deutschen Nationalbibliothek:

Die Deutsche Nationalbibliothek verzeichnet diese Publikation in der Deutschen Nationalbibliografie; detaillierte bibliografische Daten sind im Internet über http://dnb.dnb.de abrufbar.

ISBN: 9783754354018

Production and publishing: BoD - Books on Demand, Norderstedt

**Dedicated to:**

You

## What this book makes of you

When you have read this book, you will not be another person, or a better person.

Rather, **you will be even more yourself**, that "yourself" that you always wanted to be, that you have always been:

your true
free

and

unconditional **I**.

## You won't meditate all day

You won't become some kind of "Zombie" who in anything he experiences can keep calm or remain impassive, as in a state of continuous meditation... (as some might imagine meditation or spirituality).

Instead, you can enjoy every day of your life, you can do every activity, experience every emotion that life gives you....

days of glory, days of restlessness...

but in a truer way, intense, because inside you will still have the assurance that

**everything you experience is not here to destroy you.**

Who are you?

Who are you really?

You only find out by **discovering and letting go what you are not.**

## What you are not

For a moment, think about what you experienced just before you started reading this book.
A few minutes ago. You have a memory, which is more or less clear, of the past.

Then think about what you're going to do today, later, when you stop reading.
Maybe you have specific plans, maybe you don't...it doesn't matter now. You still have an idea of the future, maybe even if it' s only vague.

Now focus on what it is right now, in this moment: you are reading words in black and white... maybe you hear noises around you...

you feel the temperature in the room and of your body, you have body sensations.

Feel your breathing. If you can, breathe a couple of times more deeply than usual.

If you want, you can take a look around, around you to see the room or the place where you are now.
These are all things you can feel, which you are aware of.

Do this without judging. If you feel a judgment in yourself ("the wall is too dark") observe this "judging" from the distance of awareness in you.

As if you were witnessing to something that is happening outside of you, like something that is happening from a certain distance.

Don't identify with the judgment. In addition, you are also aware of other thoughts that maybe come to you as you read.

So not just only of things that happen on the outside, but also inside yourself as well.

As you "observe" or "hear" this, there are two entities:

1) You
2) The things you "observe"

You are not the things you observe, you are much more the awareness that "observes" these things.

Generally, however, we tend to identify ourselves with these "things": thoughts, emotions, body.

These would not be there if you were not aware of them. If you could not "observe" them. If you were not alive.

**You are this awareness, pure life.**

If you are not one of those people who is afraid of flying in an airplane, maybe this metaphor will help you.

Imagine going to the airport and being able to leave two suitcases before you get on the plane.

One suitcase is filled with the past, one with the future. Thoughts and events that have happened or imagined. Leave them and get on the plane.

On the plane you are only in the present, you are being taken from one point to another... but you don't care about it so much, you let yourself go.

There is no past or future, you can let them go for a moment.

You're not depending on the past and you don't have to worry more than necessary about the future. Only you are important now. You are alive. You are breathing. You are there. Only that matters now.

Then maybe you'll pick up those bags again, but now you're flying.

The suitcases, later, will feel lighter.

**Something useless was lost during the travel.**

Whether you're at home, on the road, or locked up in a cage:

YOU are always with you.

**YOU have not left yourself alone.**

By "YOU" I mean pure awareness of being alive. You are an expression of life.

You are not between here and there. Between past and future. Between safety and the unknown.

You are.

Beyond places and times.

You live. You breathe. Every day when you wake up. But also, while you sleep.

You are the space between all these elements apparently different and often opposite.

It breathes during the day but also at night. The unknown, the new, will be the old of the day after tomorrow.

But you are always alive.

**You breathe regardless of whether something is known or unknown.**

You are not the words you read.
You read them, but you are not a slave of
them.

You feel the temperature, it influences maybe
your mood, but you are not the temperature.

You are not your state of mind, which
changes constantly.

You are not even your thoughts. Even though
they seem to come from your mind.

You are not your mind, your mind is at your
service.

Thoughts are the result of many things you
have learned. They are not YOU. They are
information. This information can be useful,
in everyday life.

It's important to think. To change, to to plan, to solve.

But thoughts can also block you, shut you down, or lead you to do things you might regret. you might regret.

Thoughts are structures, concepts, ways of describe things that have come to you from the people who were around you. From your parents, from the people you hung out with, from the movies and commercials you saw, from the books you read.

Maybe even thoughts that you built up over time, ideas you've made your own or modified.

But again, they are just thoughts: the way your brain communicates.

Like the beats of the heart are the way the heart communicates. You are not your heart.

The heart is a part of you. Of your body. You are not just your body.

The brain is an organ at your disposal, but you are more than your brain. You can have positive, negative or neutral thoughts. They are like clouds, that dark or light pass by, and

as they come
so they will go away.

They transform, they change color, they are not stable. They are NEVER the same.

The way you thought about things or people has changed. What you think today will be tomorrow a little different and who knows in a few years.

Thoughts change like clouds, but your awareness: your conscious being that you have thoughts remains neutral and constant.

Often you are not aware of your awareness, and your thoughts direct you.

Learn to be aware of things that change, without identifying with them.

As you read these words, you relax more and more cause you move away from the dependence of, go deeper and deeper into your your being.

Go closer and closer to your awareness, to your true self, to the part in you which is the most free that there is, you are the sky that observes the clouds.

**Can the sky ever worry about some clouds, no matter how dark and threatening is?**

## You're not those trains that pass by

Your thoughts are like trains in a station...

Imagine being in this station and see the trains arriving and the trains leaving. Others are there waiting.

Some catch your attention more, they would like to take you there where you would always go, like your habits... others take you on new paths.

Some promise happiness. Others are stopped, needing to be repaired or waiting for new solutions.

For a moment, do nothing - don't choose no train. Don't let yourself get caught up in the stress of not wanting to miss an opportunity.

You can't miss out. You're there. You're here.

You can't miss the train that leads to you yourself.

Because you are here, before, during and after every experience.

You don't need that train. You have already arrived.

**Here, and wherever you will be, is your true home.**

Your thoughts and problems are on a roller coaster.

Get off.

YOU are not them. And you go farther and farther.

In the distance you always hear that noise again, and you know that at any moment you could go up and down again, but:

you don't have to now.

Now look, behind you your thoughts are maybe still on the roller coaster.
YOU have the proper distance.
You are not those emotions.
Your life is not that roller coaster.

At any time, if you want to be those emotions, you can be them. You can go back on that roller coaster.

So I'm not taking anything away from you.

Don't misunderstand me. Sometimes it's imperative to go through pain, difficulty and doubt. Sometimes certain emotions are essential.

But if you're trying to get better instantly: you have to figure out who you are, beyond of your changes and experiences, emotions however right or indispensable are.

We've gotten so used to *describing* our life (like that roller coaster) instead of *living* it.

We feel like prisoners.

If you get off instead, you can go back to living those emotions, but in a more conscious way and perhaps even more intense if this is what you wish or if this is what in this moment is indispensable.

If you must cry, cry. If you must laugh, laugh. Sometimes it is necessary to scream.

Sometimes you have to defend yourself or defend those you love.

But you won't stay on defense forever. Don't get stuck in one aspect of life or your soul

At certain times, if you feel anger, it is perhaps right to feel it, but you won't have to stay in that anger.

The less you feel compelled to identify with a passing feeling, the better you will be able to channel that feeling into something that functional, right.

**You'll know how to make the best choice in difficult times.**

## You are not the sea waves

The problems and insecurities, the news but also your thoughts are the waves of the sea.

You cannot prevent them from coming and going. As they come, they go, it's a continuous.

But you are on the beach, watching them at such a distance that you can decide in peace whether to to stay and watch them or to jump in and swim.

You don't have to do anything, now.
You can watch how the wind is blowing.
You can watch what the waves are like, high or low, fast or slow.

However the waves are:
deep in the sea or from a point on the peace is assured.

The sea in the deep is not dependent on waves or the wind.

There will also come a time to swim and enjoy the sea.

Maybe there will be a time when you have to save someone from the waves.

When you are in YOU, aware, you are not inactive. You are even more present in the present. **You KNOW when it's time to act.**

This awareness, which is ready to observe everything and the opposite of everything, is neutral.

Probably since you were in your mother's belly you were aware unconsciously of the sensations of cold or of heat, and all degrees of warmth between these extremes, just as you realized differences between dark, light...

maybe you felt differences if your mother was frrling ok  or not... every mood.

This kind of awareness, initially not capable of explaining and naming, must be neutral because the child has to learn everything and the opposite of everything.

Only later do we develop a sense of judgment, "too hot" "too little light" and so on.

So, a deeper part in you of everything else, observes without judgment the part in you that is judging.

You are not the judgment. Because everything, which you can observe, is not you.

You are the observer. You are this awareness. That observes the judgment. The judgment can change.

**Your awareness remains neutral.**
**Free. Independent.**

Inside you is like a library. Some books are still good, have information still useful, others less so, some books just are outdated.

Your subconscious is like a librarian that knows exactly where to find them.

You just tell the subconscious what the subject is, and while you relax, the subconscious goes and corrects some information.

Some old books, for example where you learned to talk, eat, walk, etc., still work. still work well.

Others, you had to read them to know things - they had a purpose then - but now those books can be put in a special display case, or in a corner of the library, or just eliminated.

They are no longer needed, no longer help, or
only partially.

There are new news, updates, an
update, that are made while you are relaxing.

Something in you, like a perfect librarian,
knows exactly what information you can get
rid of, where to find
those books, and how to change them.

**Have faith in her.**

Imagine this, a little girl has fallen into a well and is just managing to hold on somehow but by now she can hardly hold on anymore and is about to fall into the depths.

In order to get out of it, whoever wants to help her has to scratch her... otherwise she falls and dies. At that moment, the child is willing to do anything to get out.

In the same way you have lived from small things, situations that were too heavy, too dark for the little girl you were.  And then you decided to accept that help even if it wasn't exactly what you wanted, just to get out of that feeling or situation.

In your life maybe this pattern has repeated itself again and again.

You need real love, but to feel it for a moment sometimes you go beyond boundaries that you don't want to cross.

Not anymore.

You don't have to repeat this experience again. Let's look at what your true desires and boundaries you don't want to cross and what makes you feel in "a pit".

**Here is a hand that doesn't scratch you. The hand of you as an adult, saving the child.**

Maybe then you remember how, as a child, you used to enjoy pushing a ball full of air into the water.

And you would try to keep it down as much as you could...then at some point it would force itself back up.

The same happens today with your need, desire to control everything, even your emotions.

You certainly have your legitimate reasons for trying to bury, to control your emotions, but as soon as you find yourself in certain situations, you can't control them and they come back up.

So let's look instead at what that ball is filled with, why you're trying to control it, and since when.

Don't live in an attempt to control that the emotions don't come back up, help yourself or get help to understand them before this attempt to control them expands on all your actions and relationships you have.

Often you meet people who are no longer able to be open to new possibilities, new love, new perspectives because they are continually immersed in their life planning so that the old pain doesn't come back up.

But pain is like yeast, it grows behind that closed door and expands like wildfire.

**Pain can only be conquered if you deal with it in the time and measure that is right for you.**

## You are not the backpack you carry on your shoulders

Imagine for a moment that you could leave here, between these lines and words, for a couple of minutes or forever, the backpack full of stones that you have been carrying for a long time.

Imagine how you would feel. Then you can always pick it up again, later.

... maybe first you can see what to do with those rocks.

Maybe some you can shrink, color, or look at from all sides. Maybe some are less ugly or heavy than expected.

But not now, now just imagine how you look without that backpack.
Feeling free and light.
Maybe it was okay to carry it, for a time.

You did as much as you could.

"Not enough," you say, "look how weak I was at times."

Everyone needs a break.
You've done enough.

**There's something maybe you can leave here today.**

Imagine you have bought some shoes
beautiful new shoes, which you love, but the
day you you put them on you have a pebble in
your shoe.

Because you are on a date with important
people important people you don't feel like
taking it off.

You suffer for a while, then you forget about
it.

When you finally get out of that meeting, you
take off the shoe and immediately feel an
improvement, a relief,  but you realize that
your foot has almost become accustomed to it
and needs a moment to feel free again.

The foot was free, before the pebble, during
and even after.

This is your true self, beyond costume, mental constructions and judgments. and judgments:

it was free from the very beginning, before it was masked, during and after the mask.

**Your real self is free before, during and after the problems, fears, doubts.**
**It doesn't leave you.**

Imagine that one day: the little girl, the teenager, the girl you were and the woman you are, and then the old woman you will be one day ...

will dance one day hand in hand around a fire, the fire of life.

And they will know, that they were never alone.

They have always held hands and loved each other.

**They have always been there, even when it seemed not, even when someone wanted to stop it.**

With all the complications that life brings you there is only one reason in all of this: he wants to make you happy.

By happy I don't mean that you are cheerful. I mean the deep happiness of realizing that: YOU LIVE!

If you fall as a child, life wants you to learn to walk. This does not necessarily make you happy, you walk to reach beautiful but also sad places in life.

But just to LIVE, to be able to WALK, is something incredibly beautiful, a huge gift.

I had a client who suffered from multiple sclerosis, sitting in a wheelchair, and when I asked him: "but if you could walk, what would you do?"

He replied: "I would... just walk! It's such a simple thing, which I didn't know how to appreciate before, but now being able to walk would already be the greatest gift in the world!"

He gave in this way a great gift to me, because I never forget this lesson and whenever I have problems, I think of his words.

Life is not against you.
But it communicates with a code that even as children we find painful. We already wish we could do everything, understand everything. It doesn't work that way.

**If life wanted to try to make you happy, behind this harshness what would you interpret in another way and what could be the message?**

This does not excuse the seriousness of the actions of those who have unjustly harmed you.

This does not mean that you have to accept everything.

That does not mean, that it is wrong to say that you are the victim in front of a judge if someone has abused you.

That someone pays the just consequences of their unconscionable actions.

But deep down inside yourself, even though they took everything from you, you are independent and alive.

And you have the right to live again.

You have the right to be happy.

You have the right to be free.

You are like a tree, which has survived the wind, the cold, the wrong soil, the polluted water...
 ... all the evil in the world.

In spite of it all: your roots are firm, your body strong,

and your branches have learned to remain flexible. They have stretched to every corner of the sky, they have found alternative ways, solutions unimaginable before....

Stay flexible while the wind still passes. Some leaves you may still lose, but some trees live for millennial....

 ... you are like the grass of the meadow, ... when the wind passes, it seems that you are collapsing, but even if you don't have deep roots, you know how to get back up as if nothing had happened, only freed from the useless dust.

...you say, everything was taken away from you.

But when the tsunami has passed, and taken everything away, what is left?
Who are you really, when everything is taken away from you?

Now you are here, and you say, everything was taken away from you.
But these problems remained.

Now imagine that the tsunami takes everything right off you, even the problems.
But you remain, you are alive.
You have not been eliminated.

I'm not saying: long live the tsunami!

I'm saying: what you can do, who you really are, what can you start again, and what was taken away from you that was too much anyway?

Inside of you, imagine, there is like a room full of light.
It's your resources, your love, the things that make you unique...now only you know where that switch is. Only you can turn it on or off.

Now you said, that outside forces, people or situations are too negative. And you were saying, that's why you locked yourself away.

But imagine a brightly lit room. Even if around the room there is only darkness, darkness...if you open a door of the lighted room the darkness does not enter!

...rather **the light expands outside while still keeping the room lit.**

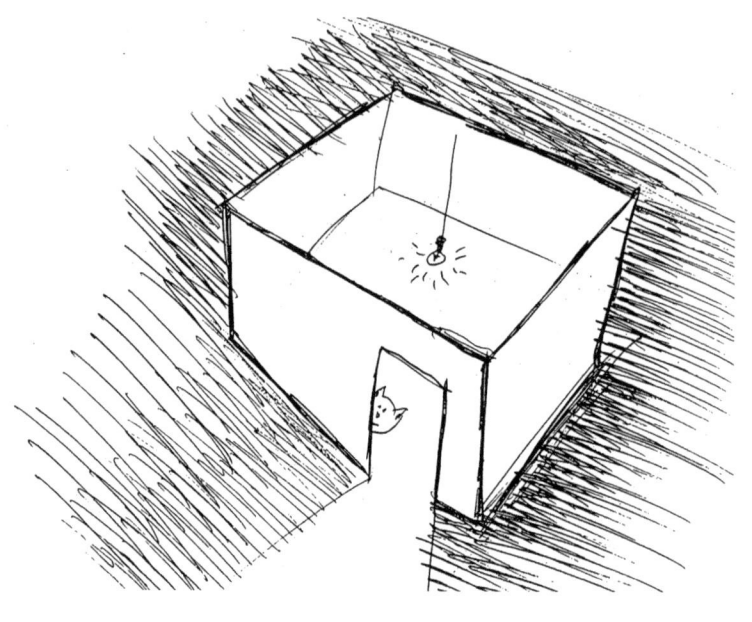

For so long you had to have the ballast
holding you to the ground, firm and secure.

Like a hot air balloon it has its own ballast.

It probably had to be that way.

But from now on, if you want, imagine
dropping those bags of ballast one by one,
detaching the ropes and flying.

Then as you fly, since you have to learn how
to use the fire that heats the balloon, maybe it
will be a little difficult at first.

Then **over time you can become the
expert.**

You often think you see a snake, but instead it's a rope.
Most of our fears have to do with the way we interpret life.

To wanting to believe our thoughts or emotions as if they are always true.

This happens because our mind is always trying to find possible dangers.

We often have good reasons, to see a danger in harmless things: experiences, traumas experienced.

A good exercise is: in quiet moments, where there are no real dangers except for some fear that comes into your mind, ask yourself:
this thought of mine, WHO receives it? And answer yourself: to ME.

# AND WHO AM I?

Maybe you won't immediately know the answer to the question: who AM I? ... but at least you will begin to find some distance between

YOU and your THOUGHTS.

As a result, you will be able to become more and more independent and decide which thoughts to believe and which not to believe.

By often asking yourself the question WHO AM I? ...

**you will arrive at a deeper truth that has nothing to do with interpretations of reality.**

## You are life

"What are you doing in life now!?" was asked
Natasha Campusch 15 years after her escape
from captivity.
 "I live," she replied.

We often forget that we are life. We are life
itself. Pure life.

One could wake up in the morning and
despite all the thoughts that are already
coming, ... remember that we are pure life.

We are proof that life exists. Not the life that
others describe or that they would like to
impose on us even by force.

Life behind life.

Life within life.

Remember that even being afraid, disillusioned or discouraged are part of life, if we were dead we would not have these feelings.

This is not a reason to prefer death to life. Rather, it is a reason to live more freely.

**To get rid of the superfluous.**

Mistakes are human. Being perfect is an illusion. The child learns to walk by making mistakes. This does not mean that if it can work, it will never stumble again.

Mistakes only remind you that you have already learned everything else.

Mistakes are the gateway to humanity, to stop wanting to be "gods or robots" who do everything right all the time. That they never make mistakes.

That they must always work.

For serious mistakes you make, of course you pay consequences or a price somewhere.

But never being wrong is impossible.

An entire Charlie Chaplin movie is based on mistakes. Small, funny coincidences and mistakes. Let them be perfectly staged.

Learn to handle your mistakes and quirks perfectly or accept them or smile about them.

So much art and so many inventions are based on mistakes.

**Perhaps humans once cooked a dish in seawater and noticed that that food tasted better with salt.**

73

Your mind is like a bodyguard, let it work as it should, don't take its place, don't do its work.

You don't have to push back the thoughts and control of the bodyguard and don't have to do its job, focus on enjoying life.

By that I mean: however your mind will be watching out for you, for possible dangers.

**You are not the bodyguard, you are the movie star now giving interviews or walking the red carpet or resting in a hotel room.**

Imagine looking for those keys that you can't find, but somewhere they are. Likewise as you search for your peace somewhere it already exists, beyond your search.

If you search or ask the wrong questions or look in the wrong places, the answers that will come to you still won't be the right ones.

That doesn't stop the right answers from being exactly where they are waiting to be discovered.

If you look for answers in things or people and situations around you, the answers might be right or wrong, deep or shallow.

If, on the other hand, it is clear to you, that the answer is you and your inner peace, all the obsessive questions in your mind or wanting to necessarily have confirmations from other people will subside.

You say: I've been sad for too many years.
Or: I've been smoking for too many years.

But if the sadness or the smoke or the suffering were to leave one day, as you would like them to, what would be left?

If you were the sadness or the smoke or the suffering, you too would leave when they leave.

Instead you will remain.

**So who are you without sadness smoke or suffering?**

Everything you think and write was different yesterday and could change tomorrow too. You are not just these thoughts. Thoughts are fortunately something that can change.

The mind should work for you, not you for it.

You are the only thing that cannot change, that cannot be influenced, that cannot be manipulated by the thoughts and actions of yourself or others.

Your body ages, your friends leave, time passes. All of this is an extraordinary sight. Even this spectacle will end one day.

**But deeper down something immortal is and remains the inexhaustible gift you have received and can always trust.**

.

You can have everything but feel an emptiness that always wants to be filled.

And there is an emptiness that does not need to be filled, because it is complete in its being free space.

There is a mind that wants to free itself from its habits and cannot do so except with great effort,

and there is a peace that does not need to free itself because it is the peace that observes the useless torture of the mind.

**There is a freedom that does not need to be defended because it was already there before the concept of freedom.**

If one recognizes that we are not our thoughts, that there is distance between my true self and my thoughts, concepts of the past, after a bit of practice, one begins to feel a kind of gratitude.

Something that tells us: yes - you have the possibility to be yourself.

You can change any negative habit overnight.

Sometimes through steps and phases. Sometimes right away, instantly.

Gratitude for a higher grace that loves us in spite of all the problems, fears and insecurities, in spite of all the negative habits and concepts that we carry around.

At the same time you may feel a kind of internal struggle, between your old self connected to the old concepts and your true self.

The old self has a very long and solid history, for which you have struggled so much, and therefore it has a hard time letting go.

In fact, for no reason in the world does it want to be erased or questioned.

It fights against your rebellion. But this conflict doesn't actually exist.

**Because the true part in you, your freedom, was there before and anyway, even before any concept was formed.**

## Conflict is an illusion

It's like the early movies, where people thought the train on the screen was going to run over them.

And instead it was just a movie.

**Our conflict is just an illusion, while the truth is relaxed and doesn't care about change.**

If joy depended on how much or what a person possessed, that is, if riches or possessions or however all the things around us gave us happiness, then the more we had the better off we would be.

Instead we all know that no person is happy unless he sleeps well.

You are pure joy, and what a joy to discover that.

**What a joy to be able to fall asleep without dilemma, to sleep well and wake up full of desire to live.**

You are love, contemplating hate.

You are forgiveness, contemplating defense.

You are the hope, contemplating despair.

You are union, which contemplates discord.
You are faith, which contemplates doubt.

You are light, which contemplates darkness.
You are life, which embraces death.
You are the true, contemplating the false.

You are the knight, who observes the dragon.
And becomes his friend.
To save the little girl princess.

**She doesn't need you to kill the dragon.
She needs to know that YOU are there.**

When all the knots that bind the heart are untied, the mortal becomes immortal. When distance cannot be reached by being together, we are reunited by being apart, for nothing is divided, all is one.

When all that seems to divide us is revealed as a magic trick, we are united.

When sadness and pain end their cycle, the opposite is revealed, which is not the opposite. Everything is one.

**When night goes out, day comes on, which is not the opposite of night but the cycle of life.**

I believe that life just tries so hard to tell us the truth. And if we don't listen, life resorts to drastic, radical solutions.

It helps us figure out in all kinds of ways what is more important, more profound, more true than what we think is true.

Discovering the truth can be so hard. But at the same time it gives us a chance to move away from an untrue view of life. And if we can glimpse this truth, despite the harshness of a situation, we move closer to true joy.

The joy of understanding our deepest truth. That we are life and we can stop wanting to be something we are not.

Life itself is this deep joy, an unbreakable joy. And we, this is what I have learned, are this. This life. This kind of joy.

Which doesn't mean being cheerful all the time, like in a commercial photo. No. And it doesn't mean being 24 hours a day in a state of meditation. It means, for me, being grateful.

**A gratitude for hidden grace, for that mystery and gift behind things, even the most terrible things.**

**Not superficially happy, not for a moment, but deep down and timeless.**

Stay open and attentive in peace as much as you can. Maybe He's already giving it to you, and you're thinking: why always me!... why always problems!

If you can tell yourself: wait a minute, what could life mean right now, what is it talking about?

... maybe an answer will come, not through thoughts, but as a silent message full of grace, like when your dog or cat approaches you and you KNOW, that they want a caress, without words.

**If you learn to listen, pain can be completely or at least partially transformed into joy.**
**Because you realize that life is on your side.**

## Endless love

We often damage ourselves in thinking:
Where to find that soul in things that in
falling in love is naturally felt....

... where one falls in love and feels miraculous
and miraculous, one would even turn water
into wine, where one sees the best in the other
person, where one tries to give the best of
oneself for the other, where one is grateful
even for the other's foibles, where one tends
to forgive anything?

But true love is a decision. I decide to love. In
spite of everything.

Something in you has decided to love you
since day zero and will not stop loving you
until the end.

Life gives you gifts all the time.
These are sometimes beautifully wrapped but
disappoint us when we open them because
our expectations are not always what life
wants from us.

Or, on the contrary, they are poorly wrapped,
like pain and suffering, but inside they hide
unexpected truths and joy.

If the gifts are not understood, life tries again,
it has to look for other ways and these can
become really unbearable and there are people
who all their lives fight against these signals,
against this way of talking about life.

I also fight often to no avail. I have fought for
years in vain.

But to go against life is to lose in the
beginning.

If I look back, I see that since I stopped
fighting with life... since I stopped wanting to
force things to go my way,

since I started listening to what life is telling
me, to understand what life wants from me...
I have been given everything I need.

**I have learned to trust.**
**And to be grateful.**

# Summary

Thank you.